The Medicine Chest

A Doctor's Prescription on Correct Usage of Medications

Dr Yatish Agarwal

जय विज्ञान JAI VIGYAN
२००४
वैज्ञानिक जागरूकता वर्ष
Year of Scientific Awareness

Rajkamal

Rajkamal Books
1-B Netaji Subhash Marg
Daryaganj, New Delhi – 110 002
Tel: 011-232 74463; 232 88769 *Fax*: 23278144
E-mail: Info@rajkamalprakashan.com

ISBN: 978-81-267-1035-5

First published in the *Year of Scientific Awareness*, 2004

This edition, 2012

Advisor
Dr Y.K. Gupta, M.D.
Professor of Pharmacology
Director, Indian Toxicological Research Centre, Lucknow

Editor : Manju Gupta
Creative Director : Abhimanyu Sinha
Graphics : Tapas Sarkar, Naresh Sharma
Production : Mahesh Chandra

The author can be reached on the e-mail at: **dryatish@yahoo.com**

₹ *60*

Printed at B.K. Offset
Shahadra, Delhi-110 032

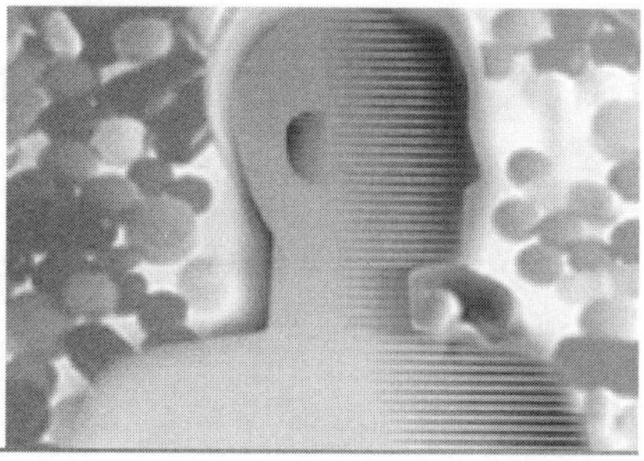

Contents

Understanding Medications

The Magic Molecules

The quest for substances that treat pain, illness, and restore health is as ancient as the human race itself. Thousands of years ago, when man expressed juice from a succulent leaf to apply to a wound, when he made alcohol and used it to ease pain, when he discovered the curative powers of roots, barks, leaves, herbs and minerals, he was well and truly on the course to discover a whole new world of medicinal substances.

The desire to take medicine is perhaps the greatest feature which distinguishes man from animals.

Sir William Osler

Opium, cannabis, cinchona, coca, foxglove, *brahmi*, *ashvagandha*, *Ma Huang*, ipecacuanha, artemesia and a number of other preparations belong to that era of primeval life. The *Rig Veda*, written between 4,000 and 6,000 BC, lists 67 medicinal compounds. The treatise left behind by Chinese scholar-emperor Shen Nung, who lived in 2735 BC, details dozens of herbal medications of his time making it one of the earliest pharmacopoeias. The ancient lands of Egypt, Sumeria, Greece, Rome, Arabia, and South and Central America, where the first human civilizations grew, were home to discovery of several medicinal substances. These discoveries, however, were limited to compounds that were found naturally in plants, animals, and minerals.

As the centuries unrolled and a new scientific order took shape, a growing understanding of chemistry soon changed the way medicines were developed. Heroin and aspirin, two of the first synthetic drugs created from other elements using chemical reactions, were produced in the late 1800s. This development, combined with the establishment of a new discipline called pharmacology—the study of medicines and their actions on the body—signalled the birth of the modern medicine industry.

New healing molecules

If the first medicines were a gift of nature, man's innocent experimentation, and serendipity, the onward march of growth and progress in pharmacology were marked by synthesis of chemical equivalents of natural biological substances and discovery of new molecules that could treat illness, protect against disease and promote better health. The crusade was to ease suffering, improve the quality of life and increase the human life span.

The last century saw a miraculous progress in the field of medicine. Deaths from many diseases, particularly those due to microorganisms, reduced drastically. Vaccines and antibiotics played a dramatic role in their eradication, prevention and control. Deadly diseases like smallpox were totally eclipsed. As a result, in the last 100 years, man's life expectancy at birth shot up from a measly 25 years to over 60, and crossed the 75-mark in developed countries.

The advent of effective drugs has brought relief to millions of people. Now, good curative medications are available against a number of major diseases. Still, there is one major stumbling block to their easy availability, and that is the price, which is high, especially when a drug is newly introduced. However, there are good reasons for this being so. The megabuck drug industry tests thousands of substances each year, of which only a few turn out to be useful enough to reach the doctor for prescribing. It requires several years from the time an idea is born in a test lab until a particular medicine wins approval and appears on pharmacy shelves. Millions of dollars go into perfecting it and making it useful.

However, as soon as the cost of research investment is recovered, and production and distribution methods improve, the price drops, often dramatically with research opening the door to more efficient and productive ways to manufacture them. You can take heart from this example. When cortisone was first introduced, its initial price was $ 200 per gram, but by 1957, it had dropped to only $2 per gram!

Designer medications

The pace of development in drug industry is very rapid. Research has opened the door to use of such novel techniques as gene splicing, or recombinant DNA, to produce new medicines. The principle involved is rather simple. The DNA of a specific type of human cell is joined to the DNA of a second organism—usually a harmless bacterium. The genetically altered organism then begins to behave just like the human cell. It begins to generate the same substance as its DNA donor cell is genetically programmed to produce. Since the bacteria multiply at a very brisk rate, drug-manufacturing companies harness them to produce the substance in large amounts. After extraction from bacteria, the substance is then purified for

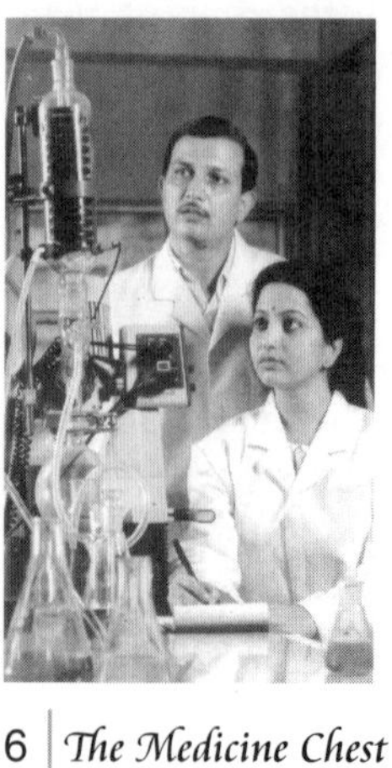

use as a medicine. Several drugs, including hormones, have been successfully produced in this manner. More are on the anvil. Researchers affirm it would not be long before designer medicinal pills become available tailor-made to suit individual requirement. They will be matched to suit the genetic structure of people. This advancement is likely make medicines more safe and effective, and curtail their adverse effects drastically.

The safety factor

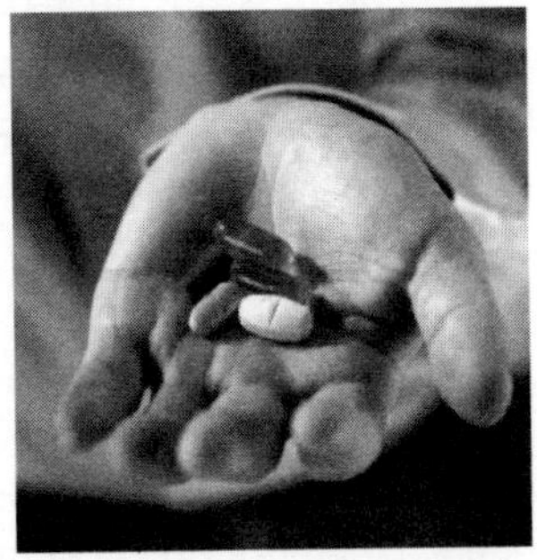

Many people deride modern-day medicines for their toxic effect on human body, and disregard them fiercely in favour of natural products. This is a curious philosophy. While it is a fact that no pharmacologically active molecule is absolutely free of potentially adverse and sometimes, serious effects, the safety record of many traditional cures is worse. Medicinal herbs, plants and metals can be toxic; their results can be unpredictable and some can prove deadly poisonous. If you go through recorded history and look at the modus operandi of assassinations, suicides, and accidental poisoning, the widespread toxicity of botanical materials and metals shall certainly not miss you.

It is equally true that some natural products are also non-toxic. The same applies to several modern-day synthetic drugs. In several cases, chemical manipulation of botanical materials has lessened the toxicity of natural alkaloids, antibiotics, hormones, snake venom, and other biological substances.

In general, the synthetic chemical molecules, currently in use in medicine, are more safe than their natural ancestors. Before being put out for the use of patients, they are put through rigorous safety tests, human trials, and only if they satisfy the safety standards are they allowed to reach the consumer. Even after their launch, they are exposed to a close and constant vigil, and if anything amiss is reported, they are immediately taken off the shelf. In comparison, the safety and therapeutic usefulness of most herbal products is often not sufficiently tested or proved, nor are any attempts made to monitor their adverse effects.

Naming medicines

Medicines can be classified and named in many ways: according to the manner they are dispensed—over the counter or by prescription; the form they are taken in—capsule, liquid, or vapour; the way they are administered—by mouth, injection, inhalation, or topical; or their action at a specific site, on a specific organ or for a specific disease. Antibiotics, for example, work against bacteria; anti-viral drugs trash viruses; amoebicidal drugs wipe out amoeba; anti-hypertensive drugs reduce blood pressure; anti-anginal drugs dilate coronaries; anti-arrhythmic drugs normalize irregular heartbeats; thrombolytic drugs dissolve blood clots; anti-epileptics reduce or eliminate seizures; tranquillizers treat anxiety; anti-depressant drugs reduce mental depression; anti-psychotic drugs alleviate the symptoms of schizophrenia; analgesic drugs reduce pain; anti-cancer drugs eliminate cancers or reduce their rapid growth and spread—the list is so long that it will fill up several pages.

Generic name and its brand names

More than the broad group or family to which a particular drug belongs, it is given a chemical name to describe its exact chemical structure. This is referred to as its generic name. Drug companies top it all by giving each medicine its own brand or trade name, by which it is popularly known in the market. Any given medicine since it is produced by a number of companies is thus sold under several brand names, and that should not confuse you. Drugs sold under generic names are equally effective as branded ones, and are cheaper by a mile.

How medicines act inside our bodies

Each medicine has to be taken in a manner that it is easily absorbed into the bloodstream. Most can be taken conveniently by mouth—that is, orally. However, those that get destroyed by the digestive juices of the stomach or intestines must be administered by another route. This is the reason insulin and several antibiotics cannot be taken by mouth.

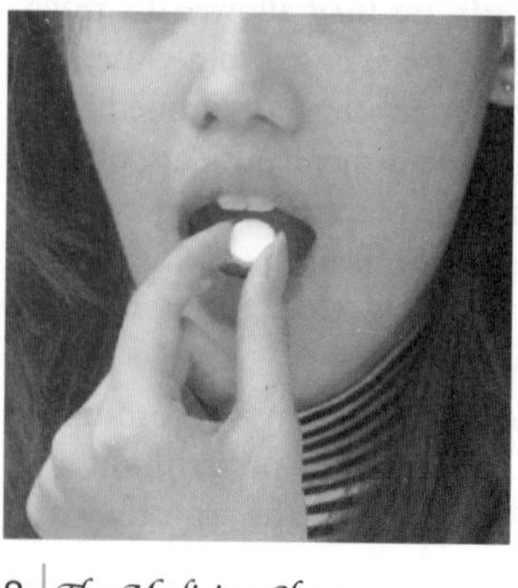

Most medicines can be injected into the body. Some are injected directly into a vein. This assures their quick dispersal through the bloodstream and a rapid effect. Others are injected into a muscle, which enables rapid absorption through the many blood vessels found in the muscle. An intra-muscular injection may also be given as a depot preparation, so that the drug is slowly released into the blood over a period of several weeks.

Some medicines are also given subcutaneously—into the tissues under the skin—like insulin. They also gradually get absorbed into the bloodstream.

A few medicines work well when inhaled. This allows them to act quickly on the lining of the nose or lungs. Typically, these include corticosteroids and bronchodilators given in bronchial asthma, and also, the anti-allergens. Some medicines are administered through drug-filled patches that stick to the skin. The medicine is slowly released from the patch and it enters the body through the skin.

Some medicines are also applied topically. While a few are used as eye- or eardrops, some are applied directly to the skin, and others are given rectally through an enema or a rectal suppository.

Whatever be the portal of entry, once a drug enters the bloodstream, it circulates to reach the site where its action is needed. Each medicine works through a different mechanism.

Many act by interacting with the body's cell receptors. Our bodies have different kinds of receptors. Each receptor has a specific chemical structure. It controls a multitude of chemical reactions and functions in the body; it is compatible only with certain medicines or endogenous compounds—substances that originate within the body such as hormones and neurotransmitters. The relationship is much like that of a lock and a key! A medicine molecule—the key—attaches itself briefly to its specific receptor—the lock—that only this molecule can open. This results in a cascade of chemical events, bringing in the intended results.

Some medicines also work by blocking specific receptors, or competing with natural chemicals that act on a particular type of receptors. For example, the beta-blocker medicines compete with adrenaline for the beta-receptors located mainly in the heart, lungs, kidneys, and blood vessels and interfere with the action of adrenaline, thus lowering the blood pressure and heart rate, preventing heartbeat irregularities and also migraine headaches.

Some medicines also modulate or suppress the body's immune response; others heal by direct action, killing bacteria, viruses, amoeba and other microbes that cause disease.

How our bodies dispose off medicines

Even as its quantity builds up to a peak therapeutic level within the body, the body begins to metabolize—break down or transform—the medicine. In the case of most medicines, it is the liver which carries out this job. In medicines which are taken by mouth, the process begins even

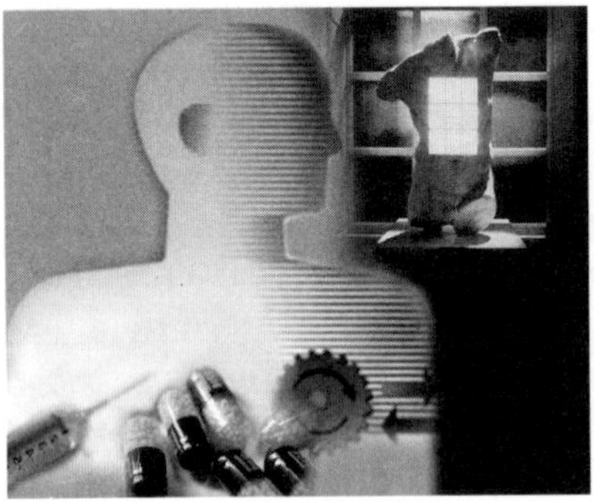

sooner! Just as the medicine molecules, after being absorbed into the bloodstream, go through the liver, the liver begins to metabolize them.

The time it takes for the blood level of a medicine to fall by 50 per cent is known as the medicine's half-life. Depending on the medicine, this can vary from a few minutes to hours or even days. It is based on a medicine's half-life that doctors determine at what frequency and at what dose an individual drug will be effective. A doctor's prescription is based on this careful scientific reasoning. By sometimes meddling with it, and not taking doses as recommended, we run into the risk of losing on the medicine's useful effect.

Each medicine and its metabolites are finally discharged, or eliminated, by the kidneys into the urine and (or) by the liver into bile, to be excreted in the faeces. Some medicines are also evaporated through perspiration or the breath.

If a person's liver or kidneys are not in good health, the metabolism and excretion of a medicine are slowed down. This requires careful consideration in selection of a medicine and sometimes neccessitates an adjustment in its dose.

Adverse reactions

A medicine can affect the body in more than one way. While it has certain desirable or beneficial effects, it can also cause undesirable harmful or adverse reactions. Some reactions, such as those that occur only in specific individuals for unexpected reasons, called idiosyncratic reactions, and those that occur with the triggering of the body's immune system, called allergic reactions, are difficult to predict. But others— those that occur because of the way a drug acts—are predictable and a person can be forewarned about them. If a side effect is serious, the medicine has to be substituted by another that is less toxic.

The decision on which drug to prescribe is based on a patient's past record with the drug, the health and age of the patient, the seriousness of his condition, and the safety profile of the drug. Medicines, such as those used to treat cancer, are known to have toxic effects; however, since the benefits outweigh the risks, they are given so that the disease may not run wild.

Taking medicines is a tricky affair. They can cause serious harm if unnecessarily and persistently used. As in other situations, abuse can cause more problems than use. Always use them with greatest care and respect, often only under a doctor's prescription. The goal is simple: their intelligent use can restore you or your loved ones to good health, quickly and effectively.

Getting the Best Out of Medicines

A Doctor's Prescription

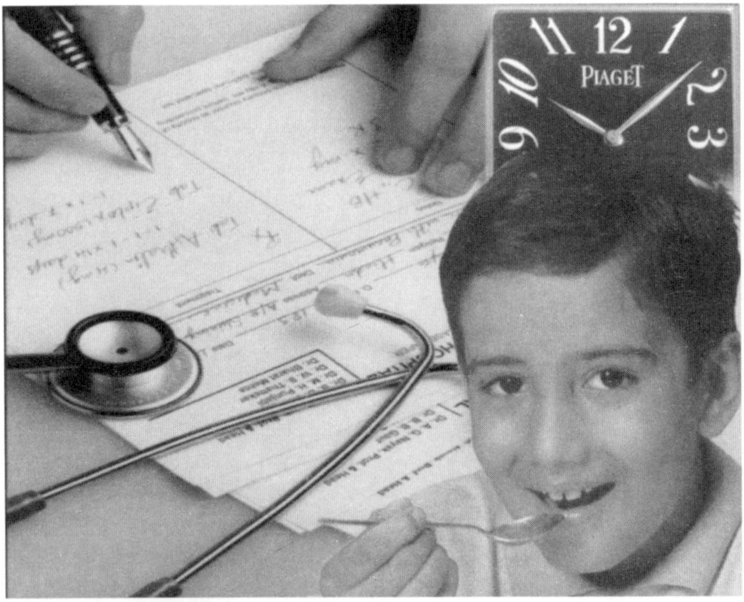

Medicines must always be used with great care. They are capable of doing a great deal of good, but if used indiscriminately, they are capable of causing serious harm. When you discuss your treatment with a physician, let him or her know if you have recently taken any other medications, including any over-the-counter (OTC) formulae, because these could affect your treatment. In addition, you should reveal if you have previously suffered any adverse reaction with any medication. If you are planning to have a baby or suspect

The Lord hath created medicines out of the earth: and he that is wise will not abhor them. Was not the water made sweet with wood, that the virtue thereof might be known?

Apocrypha
Ecclesiasticus 38:4-5

that you may already be pregnant, let your physician know. Several medicines can have harmful effects on a developing foetus.

Before starting on any medication, make sure you understand when and how to take it. Read the instructions carefully. If you do not understand anything, discuss it with the physician.

Physicians use a number of standard abbreviations while handing out prescriptions. The dosage, how and when a particular medication is to be taken, the form in which it shall be dispensed to you are coded in there. It is, therefore, always handy to know what each abbreviation stands for.

Common symbols and acronyms in a physician's prescription	
Symbols and acronyms	**What does the symbol/acronym stand for**
Symbols at the beginning of a prescription	
Δ	Doctors write their diagnosis next to this symbol.
℞	Several doctors use this symbol on the prescription. The symbol means: I write this prescription in good faith and to the best of my ability. May the good Lord cure my patient.
Acronyms specifying the frequency of dose	
o.d. (from the Latin *omni die*)	Once a day
b.d. (*bis in die*)	Twice a day (b.i.d. is sometimes used)
t.d.s. (*ter in die sumendus*)	Three times a day (t.i.d. is sometimes used)
q.d.s. (*quarter in die sumendus*)	Four times a day (q.i.d. is sometimes used)

Acronyms specifying the timing of a medication	
a.c. (*ante cibum*)	Before food
A/D	Alternate day
h.s. (*hora somni*)	At bedtime
p.c. (*post cibum*)	After food
stat. (*statim*)	Immediately
s.o.s.(*si opus sit*)	If necessary

Acronyms specifying the form of medication	
syp.	syrup
tab.	tablet
caps.	capsule
amp.	ampoule
mist.	mixture
ung. *(oint)*	ointment

Acronyms specifying the way a medicine has to be taken in	
S/L (sublingually)	A pill to be placed under the tongue
i.m. (intra-muscular)	A shot into the muscle
i.v. (intravenous)	A shot directly into a vein
s.c. (subcutaneous)	A shot underneath the skin in the tissues

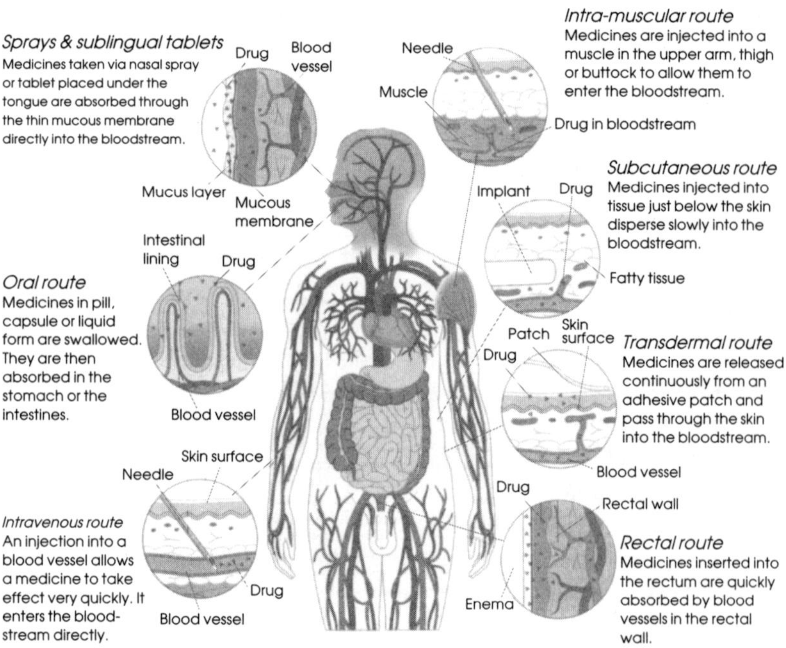

The proper use of medicines

No matter what your age or condition, it is best to adopt the following fundamental rules when taking medications:

Follow the physician's advice. Always use the medicine exactly as your physician has prescribed. An overdose or underdose, or failure to take the medicine at the prescribed intervals, can play havoc with the treatment. If you use less than the recommended dose, the medicine may lose its effect.

Space the medication properly. Devise a routine for taking the correct dose of medicine at the correct time. Space it properly. For example, if a tablet is prescribed three times a day, it implies that it has to be taken at regular eight-hour intervals—not just randomly. Even a medicine that has to be taken once daily must be taken at a fixed hour. If a person is careless about the timing of a medicine, there would be periods when blood levels would dip too low, and the medicine would lose its effect.

Never rush. When taking tablets or capsules, swallow them with plenty of water so that they do not become stuck in your food-pipe. If you are taking liquid medicine, shake the bottle before use to mix the ingredients well, and measure the doses carefully.

Time your dose with meals. In general, medicines are best taken with meals. This helps in the absorption of medicines that are soluble in fat, and also protects against their irritant effect on stomach.

Some medicines, however, are best taken at least an hour before or two hours after a meal since a full stomach may hamper their absorption. Anti-histamines taken to quell allergies, ACE inhibitors like Captopril, Enalapril, Lisinopril and Quinapril which work as anti-hypertensives, or anti-tubercular medicines like rifampicin, or Penicillamine usually taken for rheumatoid arthritis and Wilson's disease, and most oral antibiotics fall under this group. In contrast, medicines taken to check nausea and vomiting are best swallowed at least half an hour before eating, while antacids work well if taken an hour after meals.

You should also check if a particular food is taboo with your medication. Several food-medication interactions may not only nullify the medication, but may lead to serious accidents, though rarely does it happens so.

Do not stop midway. Make sure that you complete the full course of any treatment. Even if your symptoms lessen or disappear, do not stop the medication without consulting your physician. If you stop midway, the disease can sometimes get worse. This is particularly true of infections like tuberculosis, which needs a treatment of six to nine months or more.

Inform your physician of side effects. Be alert to headache, dizziness, blurred vision, ringing in your ears, shortness of breath, hives or any other unexpected effects. Seek medical help if you develop any unexpected symptom that seems unrelated to your illness while taking medicines. If you have a severe reaction to a medicine, such as difficulty in breathing, call for urgent medical attention. If you have a mild reaction from a prescribed medicine, see your physician as soon as possible and ask whether you should stop the treatment.

Keep a record of allergies. If you develop an allergy or intolerance to any medication, make a written note of it in your diary, or PC, or laptop. Let your physician know and be careful about not taking that medication again.

Store medicines properly. Keep medications safe. Most medicines require a dry, secure place at room temperature and out of direct sunlight. Some need refrigeration. The medicine cabinet should be kept out of the reach of small children. If the cabinet cannot be kept out of their reach, it should be fastened securely by lock, and the key kept at a place accessible only to adults.

Keep the label safe. Keep medicines in their original containers. If the label gets separated from a medicine container and there is any doubt regarding its contents, dispose of the medicine immediately.

Discard outdated drugs. Medicine deteriorates over time and can sometimes become toxic. Never take a medicine the expiration date of which has lapsed. While easing out tablets out of a strip, be careful to use the end where the expiry date is printed last.

Don't take any medication in the dark. This may lead to accidents and poisoning. Time after time mistakes are made and a dangerous or wrong drug is taken leading to a serious emergency.

Taking long-term medication. If you need medical treatment that continues for a long time, such as medication to treat high blood pressure, or diabetes mellitus, see the doctor regularly so that he or she can monitor your condition and your response to treatment. Do not automatically keep repeating the medication without knowing if it is doing its job or not.

Do not stop taking your medication without consulting your physician first. If you run into any other illness and need to treat that, it is best to checkout with your physician. Some medicines can interact with others, and cause a change in their effective level. Some medicines, such as anticoagulants, can cause problems during surgery or emergency treatment.

The emergency medical staff must be given the details of your medication. This information is absolutely vital.

Avoid mixing medications and alcohol. This combination can cause a harmful interaction. The effect of many medications is either boosted or hampered by alcohol, and some may also react dangerously.

Giving medicines to children. Medicines for babies and toddlers usually comes in liquid form, which is easier for them to swallow. It is normally simpler to administer liquid medicine by a syringe or a dropper. A child who strongly dislikes medicine can hold his or her nose while taking it. Have a pleasant drink ready to wash away the taste afterwards.

Never lend or share medicines or self-medicate. What helps you might harm others. Often, symptoms can be confusingly similar and deceptive because the same symptom can arise from many causes. It is not logical to use medicines without clearly understanding what the problem is. Reactions to medicines differ with different people, and in the same person at different times and under different conditions; therefore, all medicines are prescribed with careful thought. A physician has knowledge, wisdom, and practical experience based on which he decides the treatment. If he feels unsure, he first investigates the patient, comes to a diagnosis, and only then begins the treatment.

Often, minor conditions improve with or without treatment. Therefore, if you do well with self-medication, do not pat your back. You could be plain lucky, or downright silly, since the ailment would have cleared without the help of any medication.

Some Mix-ups You Could Do Without

Food-Drug Interactions

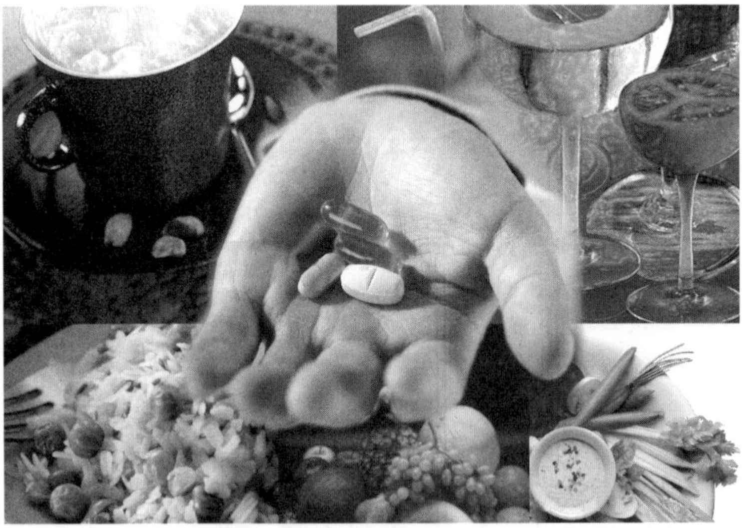

Would it occur to you not to swallow a tetracycline capsule or a particular antibiotic pill with a glass of milk? Or to avoid alcohol if you are taking a certain medicine to overcome amoebiasis? Or not eat citrus fruits, pickles, and acidic foods if you are taking erythromycin? Probably not! Nevertheless, these are just some of the food-drug interactions that you should be careful about.

Several foods can affect the function of modern-day medications. While some only hinder certain medications from doing their job, others can cause downright dangerous reactions and trigger a sudden medical crisis.

In order to live a fully human life we require not only control of our bodies; we must touch the unity and resonance of our physicality, our bond with the natural order, the corporeal grounds of our intelligence.

Adrienne Rich
Of Woman Born

Some foods contain natural or added chemicals that can react with certain medicines in ways that render the latter virtually useless. For example, the calcium in dairy products can knock out tetracyclines and quinolones. Acid fruit or vegetable juices can quash erythromycin and oral penicillin. Liquorice (*mulethi*), a favourite ingredient of candy and a commonly used flavouring agent, can counteract the effect of high blood pressure medications. The list can go on and on!

But that's not the only way foods affect medications. Just the simple presence of food in the digestive tract can also sometimes slow down or enhance the absorption of a drug from the stomach. All anti-histamine allergy pills, anti-hypertensive ACE inhibitor medications—enalapril, lisinopril and quinapril, anti-tubercular medicine—rifampicin, and many oral antibiotics find food a hindrance to their entering the bloodstream. However, the presence of certain foods also speeds up the absorption of some medications. For example, blood levels of griseofulvin, a drug which fights ringworm, rise markedly if a fat-rich meal is taken before swallowing the medication. If you wish to know more about such mix-ups, here is a list you could refer to:

Check, if you're taking any of these drugs	If yes, avoid the listed foods!	What is the necessity of taking this safety measure?
Anti-amoebic medicine		
Metranidazole	Avoid alcohol until three days after you stop the medication.	Alcohol does not mix well with metranidazole. A serious interaction can occur causing nausea, abdominal cramps, vomiting, headaches and flushing.

Check, if you're taking any of these drugs	If yes, avoid the listed foods!	What is the necessity of taking this safety measure?
Antibiotics		
Tetracycline Doxicycline Minocycline	Avoid calcium-containing foods like milk, yoghurt, cheese; vitamin-mineral supplements containing iron; and, antacids.	Presence of calcium, aluminium or iron interferes with the intestinal absorption of tetracycline and lets it go waste.
Erythromycin Penicillin-V	Avoid acidic foods: citrus fruits, tomatoes, pickles, vinegar, fruit juices, colas, coffee and tea.	Increased stomach acidity can destroy these antibiotics.
Quinolones Ciprofloxacin Levofloxacin Ofloxacin	Take preferably on an empty stomach 1 hour before or 2 hours after a meal. Avoid calcium-containing foods like milk, yoghurt, cheese; vitamin-mineral supplements containing iron; antacids; coffee, colas and tea.	This facilitates better absorption of the medicine. These foods and supplements significantly decrease the drug concentration.
Anti-fungal medicines		
Ketaconazole	Avoid alcohol while taking ketaconazole and until the next three days after you stop the medication.	Alcohol does not gel with ketaconazole. A serious interaction can occur causing nausea, abdominal cramps, vomiting, headaches, flushing and sudden drop in blood pressure.
Griseofulvin Fluconazole Ketaconazole Itraconazole	Avoid calcium-containing foods like milk, yoghurt, cheese; and antacids.	Presence of calcium, aluminium or magnesium interferes with the intestinal absorption of anti-fungal agents.

Check, if you're taking any of these drugs	If yes, avoid the listed foods!	What is the necessity of taking this safety measure?
Blood pressure-lowering medications		
Anti-hypertensive medications	Liquorice (*mulethi*)	Regular intake of liquorice increases blood pressure and reduces the efficacy of anti-hypertensive medicines.
ACE inhibitors Captopril Enalapril Lisinopril Quinapril	Avoid eating large amounts of foods high in potassium such as bananas, green-leafy vegetables, and oranges.	ACE inhibitors increase the amount of potassium in our body. By taking foods rich in potassium, the potassium level in the body can rise to a hazardous level.
Beta blockers Atenolol Metoprolol Propranolol	Avoid alcohol.	The combination may lower the blood pressure drastically.
Medications for angina		
Nitrates Isosorbide dinitrate Nitroglycerin	Avoid alcohol.	Avoid alcohol because it may add to the blood vessel-relaxing effect of nitrates and result in dangerously low blood pressure.
Diuretic medicines		
Triamterene (Ditide), Spironolactone, and Amiloride	Avoid eating large amounts of potassium-rich foods such as bananas, oranges and green leafy vegetables, or salt substitutes that contain potassium.	Potassium-sparing diuretics block the excretion of potassium. This can push up the potassium inside the body. Excess of potassium can cause irregular heartbeat.
Cholesterol-lowering medications		
Atorvastatin Lovastatin Simvastatin	Avoid alcohol.	Taking large amounts of alcohol increases the risk of liver damage.

Check, if you're taking any of these drugs	If yes, avoid the listed foods!	What is the necessity of taking this safety measure?
Anti-coagulants (blood-thinning agents)		
Coumadin Dicumarol Warfarin	Foods high in vitamin K e.g., leafy green vegetables, potatoes, and liver.	Consumption of foods high in vitamin K may counteract the blood-thinning effect of anticoagulant medicines.
Coumadin	Vitamin E supplements.	High doses of vitamin E (400 IU or more) may prolong clotting time and increase the risk of bleeding.
Thyroid medications		
Thyroxin	Soyabeans, turnips, cabbage, Brussels sprouts, and kale.	These foods contain goitrogens—substances which inhibit production of the thyroid hormone. They can, therefore, worsen goitre.
Anti-anxiety pills		
Diazepam Alprazolam Lorazepam	Avoid alcohol	Alcohol further impairs mental and motor performance increasing the risk of accidents during driving.
	Coffee, tea and cola drinks	Lessen the anti-anxiety effects of these drugs.
Anti-depressants		
MAO inhibitors Phenelzine Tranylcypromine	Avoid alcohol; soya sauce; miso soup; bananas; processed Cheddar, mozzarella cheese; yoghurt; sour cream; yeast extracts; raisins; cured meats such as sausage and salami; beef or chicken liver; dried fish; ginseng; caffeine-containing products.	A rapid, potentially fatal spurt in blood pressure and brain haemorrhage can occur if alcohol or foods containing tyramine are consumed with MAO inhibitors.

Check, if you're taking any of these drugs	If yes, avoid the listed foods!	What is the necessity of taking this safety measure?
Anti-histamines (anti-allergic pills)		
Cetirizine Clemastine Loratadine Chlorpheniramine Diphenhydramine	Avoid alcohol.	Some anti-histamines may cause drowsiness and slow your mental and motor performance. Exercise caution while driving or operating a machine.
Fever and pain relief pills		
Paracetamol	Avoid alcohol.	Chronic alcohol use can increase your risk of liver damage.
Aspirin Ibuprofen Naproxen Diclofenac	Avoid or limit the use of alcohol.	Alcohol use can increase your risk of stomach bleeding and liver damage.
Corticosteroids (Inflammatory, allergic and auto-immune disorders)		
Prednisolone Betamethasone Dexamethasone	Avoid alcohol.	Can cause erosions in the stomach and sometimes, even bleeding.
Oral anti-diabetic pills		
Metformin, Chlorpropamide and others	Avoid alcohol.	Serious interactions can occur causing dangerously adverse reactions.
Bronchodilators (asthma, bronchitis)		
Theophylline	High-carbohydrate foods.	High carbohydrate foods decrease absorption.
Theophylline	Avoid alcohol.	Taking alcohol increases the risk of side effects: nausea, vomiting, headache, irritability.
Theophylline Albuterol Epinephrine	Avoid eating or drinking large amounts of foods and beverages that contain caffeine (e.g. chocolate, colas, coffee, tea).	Both oral bronchodilators and caffeine stimulate the central nervous system

Ways to avoid conflicts between food and medications

Here are a few simple *mantras*:

- Do not swallow any medication with fruit juice, carbonated beverages, or caffeine drinks; use a full glass of ordinary drinking water.
- To be on the safe side, take a complete holiday from alcohol.
- Follow your physician's advice about when to take medication and what foods or beverages to avoid.
- Read the labels on over-the-counter remedies and the package inserts.

Medications and nutrition

Just as foods affect medication, some medicines also can adversely affect the body's nutrition. While a few hinder absorption of certain nutrients, some interfere with the body's ability to convert nutrients into usable forms, and others hasten excretion of certain nutrients. This nutrient depletion occurs gradually, but for those taking long-term medication these interactions can have a significant bearing on health.

Medications that cause nutritional deficiencies

Medicine	Nutrient deficiency
Deficiencies occurring due to hindrance in absorption	
Anti-epileptics	
Phenobarbital	Calcium, folic acid
Diphenylhydantoin	Calcium, folic acid
Laxatives	
Mineral oil	Carotene, vitamins A, D, K
Corticosteroids	Calcium
Neomycin	Fat, lactose, sodium, potassium, calcium, iron, vitamin B_{12}
Antacids	Phosphorus
Tetracycline	Calcium, magnesium, vitamin B12
Azulfidine	Folic acid
Deficiencies caused by inability of the body to use nutrients	
Oral contraceptives	Folic acid, riboflavin, vitamin $B_{6,}$ vitamin C, copper
Anti-cancer medication	
Methotrexate	Folic acid
Anti-bacterial and anti-malarial	
Pyrimethiamine	Folic acid

Diuretic	
Triamterene	Folic acid
Anti-tubercular medicines	
Isoniazid	Vitamin B_6
Pyrazinamide	
Ethionamide	
Anti-hypertensive	
Hydralazine	Vitamin B_6
Parkinson's disease	
L-dopa	Vitamin B_6
Arthritis, Wilson's disease	
Pencillamine	Vitamin B_6
Anti-coagulant	
Coumarin	Vitamin K

Deficiencies caused by increased loss in urine

Aspirin	Vitamin C
Antibiotic	
Gentamycin	Magnesium, calcium, potassium
Diuretic	
Thiazides	Magnesium, potassium, sodium, zinc
Furosemide	Potassium, sodium, zinc, calcium
Anti-tubercular medicine	
Isoniazid (INH)	Vitamin B_6
Heart medicine	
Digitalis	Calcium, Magnesium
Anti-cancer drug	
Cisplatin	Magnesium

How to prevent nutritional deficiencies?

You might ask how you can prevent these deficiencies—the answer is not always simple. However, here are a few suggestions:

- If your physician writes a vitamin or a mineral supplement, do not ignore it. There are times when nutritional supplements are necessary.
- Eat a nutritionally well-balanced diet. Use of a needed drug, even on a long-term basis, is less likely to cause depletion of vitamins and minerals if your overall nutritional status is good.
- Do not make a habit of swallowing even seemingly harmless medication like an antacid or a laxative. They can also compromise your nutritional status.

Popular Beliefs about Medications

Facts and Fables

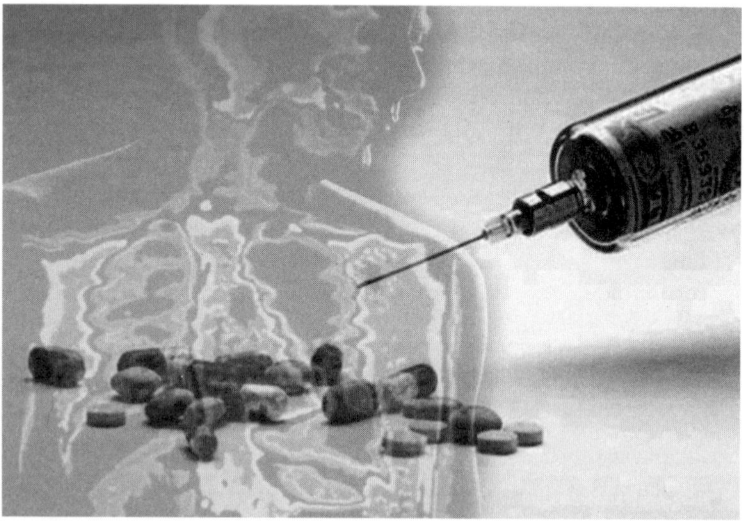

Just as in any other walk of life, myths about medications also bestride our social order. They express and confirm our cultural attitudes, our values, and our past experiences, which over time acquire a pedestal of permanence in our minds. If once a medicine shot came in handy to diffuse a medical crisis, or a few bottles of glucose instilled life into a dehydrated person, or a medicine led to a disastrous adverse effect, the image remains entrenched in our minds and takes on a special meaning, but all that meets the eye is not always the

I therefore claim to show, not how men think in myths,
but how myths operate in men's minds without
their being aware of the fact.

Claude Lévi-Strauss
The Raw and the Cooked

truth. Let us go over some of the more common facts and fables that colour the world of medications.

Shots, pills and capsules

Syringes and needles carry a magical significance for some people. They believe that where 'ordinary' pills and capsules fail, shots can cure. But that's wrong. Shots, pills, capsules, liquid, creams, or sprays are merely a form to introduce different medications into the body. Medicine given in any form eventually enters the bloodstream and circulates to reach the site where its action is needed. Non-oral forms, such as inhaled and injected medicines, have the advantage of more rapid action since they bypass the digestive system; but each form has its own drawbacks and advantages.

Tablets and liquids hold a major advantage as they are easy to take. Unlike syringes and needles, they also do not carry any risk of infection. A shot causes discomfort and pain, requires the services of a nurse or doctor, and can sometimes excite an infection, abscess or severe disabling pain if the drug is accidently injected into a nerve root. Injectables also cause more severe adverse reactions than oral preparations.

However, injectable medicines also have their use in certain special situations. Some medicines cannot be taken by mouth since they are destroyed by the digestive juices in the stomach. A classical example is insulin. Take another situation: a person is unconscious or has an obstruction in the throat. He or she cannot be given anything by mouth. In such a setting, intravenous and intra-muscular shots can be the only way to administer a medication. Also when over an immediate drug effect is needed, an intravenous injection works best since it ensures a rapid delivery of the drug.

The bottom line is: extract the maximum benefit out of medication with as little risk as possible.

The heat index

The belief that allopathic medicines cause severe dryness in the body is very popular. People cite different facts to buttress this thought: change in colour of urine, a feeling of heat and warmth in the body, or dryness of mouth and throat. Yet, the truth is, these effects cannot be generalized to all drugs employed by modern medicine, nor are these a representative of any heat reaction in the body. Rather, they occur as part of a simple physical process or predictable side effects because of the known chemical effects of a medication.

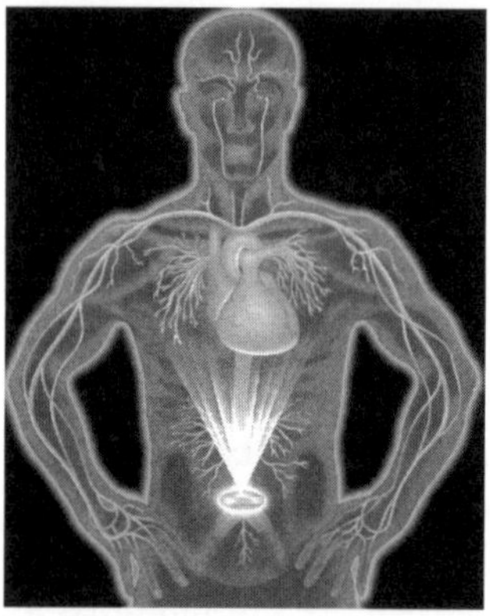

Medicines that are discharged or eliminated in the urine deepen its colour. Vitamin supplements colour the urine deep yellow, anti-tuberculous medicine, Rifampicin, colours it red or deep pink, while Nitrofurantoin can colour it brown. Nitrates cause dilation of blood vessels, and for that reason, lead to a sudden feeling of warmth. Anti-histamines and tricyclic anti-depressants, because of their chemical effect, lead to dryness of mouth. The heat index of a medicine is nowhere in the picture.

The less, the better

Many people think physicians write too many medicines and prescribe them in too high doses. Guided by this belief, they halve the prescribed dose of a medication and then feel perturbed if the treatment fails.

The fact is the frequency and dosage of each medication is guided by sound pharmacological principles, and not by a doctor's whims or fancies. The quantity of a drug must reach an optimum level in the body, and this level must be maintained round-the-clock for it to show its therapeutic effect. Further, since the body begins to metabolize the medication as soon as it enters blood stream, each medication only has a certain finite life in the body. This can vary between different medicines from a few minutes to hours or even days. A doctor bases his advice on this sound scientific basis, and therefore, the dosage that he writes brooks no meddling. The next time you feel like halving your doctor's prescription, remember this simple fact.

The withering effect

Do you believe that if you take a medication for a long time, your body adapts to it and the drug loses its efficacy? Many people do, and they could be right! With some medications, the body does develop a tolerance towards them. While this may make a medication less effective over time, and to obtain the same result, it may become obligatory to switch to a higher dose, or sometimes makes a change in medication inescapable, this should never be a pretext for you to stop a medication on your own.

Treatment for high blood pressure, diabetes and other chronic illnesses requires a continuous drug therapy often for life. If you are careful and visit your physician on a regular basis, the withering effect can be taken care of by introducing suitable timely changes in the prescription.

In contrast, continuous use of some medications is fraught with risk. You may get hooked to them. The dependence, may be psychological—you may feel you cannot function normally without it. Or it may be physical—your body becomes so dependant that you develop physical symptoms if you stop the drug. The bottom line is: do not abuse drugs; just follow your doctor's advice.

The ultimate medicine

If you feel weak, easily fatigued or have become anaemic, is running an infusion of a little of glucose the ultimate remedy? Thought to be the final remedy by many, a bottle of glucose is only as good as its name suggests. It contains fluid which carries 5, 10 or more per cent

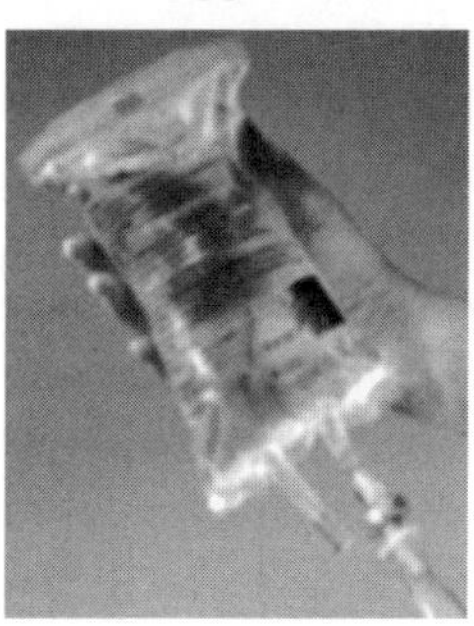

glucose; nothing else of note. The recipe can be life saving for a person who is dehydrated, but has no special curative or nutritional significance for a normally hydrated person. You can actually obtain the same benefit by buying a glucose packet, mixing it in water and drinking the produce. Eating some fruits can even work better. Why then clamour for a bottle of glucose, remain hooked to it and pay through your nose?

Claims and falsehoods

Quackery in medicine probably is as old as, if not older than, civilized man. It was Voltaire who said that the quack was born when the first knave met the first fool. There are many advertisers and individuals who claim they have special products which can increase height, shape up the body, enhance one or the other body curves or anatomical parts, and cure and treat infertility, assure a baby boy, or even treat such organic diseases as cancer, arthritis, high blood pressure and diabetes by a special method or by a certain product which can be bought over the counter at a herbal store or as a mail order! Curiously, not just the illiterate, even the educated fall into the trap of such false assurances, which are made with the sole objective of making a quick buck. There are no ethics or concern for the people who become victims of this fraud.

You should simply apply your mind before trying out such treatments. If remedies and cures such as those advertised did exist, modern medicine would have been keen to spot them and accept them into its fold. A score of medications, including digitalis, reserpine, quinine, have been acquired from folk remedies.

Safety of herbs and traditional medicines

Herbal treatments, ayurveda and other traditional treatments have existed for many centuries. Those who practise these systems of medicine often strongly argue about the safety and effectiveness of their medicines and deride those of allopathic drugs. While there is no doubt that ayurveda has much to offer and—even if some of its fundamentals are not based on any scientific evidence—it has benefited the human race for the past hundreds of years, it is naïve to believe that herbs, metals and potions that ayurveda and other traditional systems of medicine use are safe and harmless for the human body.

The fact of the matter is: no medicine can be absolutely safe, not even natural herbs and produce. Do you think hemp, tobacco, marijuana, and cocaine are harmless? After all, they all grow in nature. Heavy metal poisoning is also rather common with serious toxic effect on the kidneys and liver. Not that this should detract one from the strengths of ayurveda, but a more rational approach can be its best ally in development and growth.

Medicine Chest

Common Medicines: Benefits and Safeguards

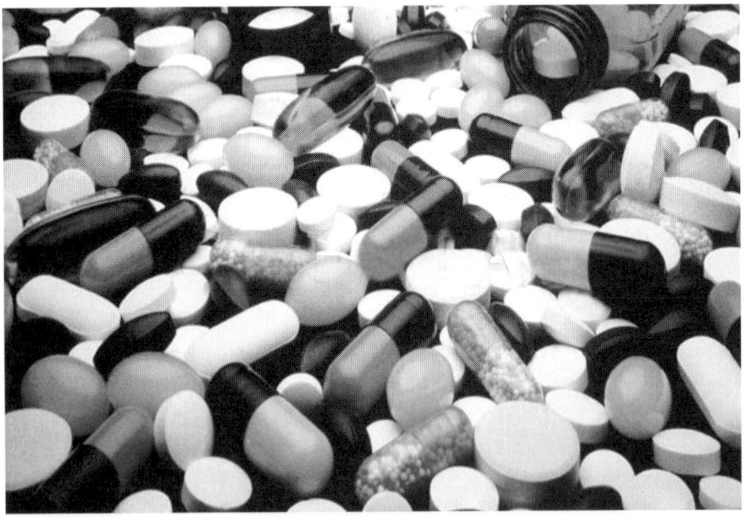

From a handful of proven medications a hundred years ago to the several hundred available today, the 'medicine chest' has expanded in a major way. A wide range of medicines is now at hand to cure, alleviate, diagnose, or prevent disease. To make their best use, it helps to know the basics. Understanding how different medications work, and how to use them safely and effectively makes it easier to meet the goal.

Anti-infective Drugs

Anti-infective drugs are a group of medications used primarily to treat infections caused by various microbes. They are classified

Even diseases have lost their prestige, there aren't so many of them left.... Think it over....no more syphilis, no more clap, no more typhoid.... antibiotics have taken half the tragedy out of medicine.

Louis-Ferdinand CéLine

as anti-bacterials, anti-virals, anti-amoebics and anti-fungals depending on the type of microbe they combat.

Anti-bacterial medicines and antibiotics

Anti-bacterial medicines and antibiotics are among the most commonly prescribed medicines in the world. They are used to treat and prevent bacterial infection. They act by interfering with some specific characteristics of bacteria. For example, they may destroy bacterial cell walls or interfere with the synthesis of bacterial proteins or deoxyribonucleic acid (DNA)—the chemical that carries the genetic material of an organism. Some kill bacteria directly, while others halt their multiplication. Based on their chemical composition and the way in which they work, they are classified into different groups.

Major Antibiotics: *Penicillins:* Ampicillin, Amoxycillin, Cloxacillin, Penicillin-V; *cephalosporins:* Cephalexin, Cefazolin, Cefadroxyl, Cefuroxime, Cefaclor, Ceftazidime, Cefipime, Cefuroxime; *quinolones:* Ciprofloxacin, Levofloxacin, Norfloxacin, Ofloxacin, Sparfloxacin, Gatifloxacin; *aminoglycosides:* Streptomycin, Gentamicin, Neomycin, Tobramycin, Amikacin; *macrolides:* Erythromycin, Roxithromycin, Azithromycin, Clarithromycin; *tetracyclines:* Tetracycline, Doxycycline, Minocycline; *sulphonamides:* Co-trimoxazole, Sulphadiazine; *others*: Chloramphenicol, Metronidazole, Clindamycin, Trimethoprim, Vancomycin etc.

Benefits: Useful against all kinds of infections—of the skin, ear, throat, lungs, bones, joints, urinary tract or any tissue or organ in the body, they can act their part as life saviours in life-threatening infections such as septicaemia and bacterial meningitis.

Safeguards: Antibiotics often cure an infection completely. However, bacteria can spontaneously mutate, producing strains that are resistant to existing antibiotics. This especially happens if you leave the treatment midway, as soon as you feel better. The dictum is: when you are taking antibiotics, take the entire course as prescribed by your doctor. This is important in order to eradicate the infection.

If you have epilepsy, liver or kidney disease, some antibiotics may not be safe. Let your doctor know if you suffer from any other major illness than the current one for which you seek the cure. Tetracyclines can cause changes to growing bones and teeth and are therefore not suited to young children or pregnant women. Quinolones can cause convulsions and should not be taken by people with epilepsy.

Drug interactions: Several antibiotics do not gel with other treatments. Antacids can reduce the absorption of tetracyclines; Erythromycin can push up Bromocriptine to toxic levels, while Amoxycillin and Co-trimoxazole can accentuate the effect of anti-coagulants increasing the risk of haemorrhage.

Side effects: The most common side effect with antibiotics is diarrhoea, although it is not usually severe. Their long-term use can cause overgrowth of the yeast *Candida albicans* in or on the body. Some people develop rashes since they are sensitive to a particular antibiotic. At other times, a life-threatening allergic reaction known as anaphylaxis may occur, particularly with injectable penicillin. Some people who are allergic to penicillin may also be allergic to cephalosporins. If you have an adverse reaction, such as a rash, stop taking the medicine and call your doctor immediately.

Aminoglycosides can sometimes affect the sense of hearing and balance, damage the kidneys, and cause severe skin rashes. Sulphonamides can also cause serious side effects, including kidney damage. Chloramphenicol can suppress the bone marrow, and that can be dangerous. It must therefore be only used when it is needed most, such as in typhoid.

Anti-tuberculous drugs

Tuberculosis is a major public disease caused by the bacillus, *Mycobacterium tuberculosis*. It usually occurs in the lungs, but may also affect other parts of the body, such as the lymph nodes, digestive tract, kidneys, and sometimes the membranes covering the brain and spinal cord. Anti-tuberculous medicines can help eliminate the infection.

Major medicines: Isoniazid, Rifampicin, Ethambutol, Pyrazinamide, Streptomycin, Cycloserine, Capreomycin, Kanamycin, Ciprofloxacin, Ofloxacin, Ethionamide.

Safeguards: Anti-tuberculous treatment is of long duration. In general, a full course of treatment takes six to nine months, but it can even take up to 12-18 months, depending on the organs that are affected. You should never stop the treatment the moment you begin to feel better. If you fail to complete the treatment, the tubercular bacilli may mutate, and drug-resistant strains may appear which are extremely hard to treat.

Pyridoxine supplements are a must with Isoniazid. Else, a deficiency may occur affecting the nerves, which causes numbness or tingling in the hands or feet. Rifampicin is best taken before breakfast. This helps in its absorption.

Drug interactions: Rifampicin can weaken the effect of oral contraceptive pills, anti-fungal pills, anti-diabetic agents, anti-epileptics, anti-coagulants and a number of other medicines. You should therefore check with your physician before taking any other medicine.

Side effects: Anti-tuberculous medicines may produce various side effects, including nausea, vomiting, rashes, and abdominal pain. Isoniazid, Rifampicin and Pyrazinamide may damage the liver or kidneys; your doctor will regularly check your liver and kidney function. Rifampicin may turn urine and other body secretions, red, but this effect is harmless. Ethambutol may damage the nerves in the eyes, causing vision problems, though this occurs rarely. If you are taking Ethambutol and develop blurred vision, see your doctor promptly. Streptomycin, now less used, can affect the sense of hearing and balance.

Anti-viral drugs

Anti-viral medicines act to control the virus by preventing its entry into a host cell or by blocking its replication. Anti-viral medicines may cure, but often only suppress, viral infections; and flare-ups of an infection can occur after symptom-free periods. With some viruses, such as human immunodeficiency virus (HIV), anti-viral medicines can only prolong life; not cure the disease.

Major medicines: Acyclovir, Amantadine, Didanosine, Efaviranez, Famciclovir, Idoxuridine, Indinavir, Interferon, Lamvudine, Neviparine, Ribavarin, Stavudine, Zidovudine.

Benefits: Anti-viral medicines are used to treat recurrent attacks of cold sores in the mouth and genital herpes, chickenpox as well as shingles caused by varicella-zoster virus, chronic active hepatitis due to hepatitis B and C viruses, influenza, and HIV/AIDS.

Drug interactions: Some anti-histamines and sleeping tablets can react with Indinavir and cause serious problems. One should not take oral contraceptive pills with Neviparine. Concomitant prolonged use of Zidovudine and Paracetamol can lead to defficiency of neutrophil white blood cells. Such risky combinations are best avoided.

Side effects: When taken orally, Acyclovir may cause nausea. Rarely, it may lead to fatigue, confusion and seizures. Amantadine causes reactions such as dizziness, confusion, and insomnia. Interferon commonly produces side effects, including nausea and flu-like symptoms such as tiredness, fever, and aching muscles. These effects are usually mild and may diminish with continued treatment. Prolonged treatment can sometimes lead to decreased production of red and white blood cells. In a few cases, people taking Interferon may develop tremors. Stavudine and Zidovudine can cause headache and nausea, and sometimes, sleeplessness and flu-like symptoms.

Anti-malarial drugs

Malaria is a parasitic disease caused by plasmodium. The infection is transmitted to humans by the bites of infected mosquitoes. The parasite travels through the blood to the liver, where it multiplies before re-entering the blood and circulating throughout the body. At this stage, the symptoms of malaria appear.

Major anti-malarials: Chloroquine, Primaquine, Mefloquine, Proguanil, Sulphadoxime-Pyrimethamine combination, Pyrimethamine, Quinine, Arteether, Artesunate, Artemether.

Benefits: Some anti-malarial medications can be used for both prevention and treatment. Others can be used only for treatment of the infection.

Safeguards: If you have epilepsy, you should avoid Chloroquine and Mefloquine. People who have a congenital deficiency of G 6-PD enzyme in the blood cells should not take Primaquine.

Drug interactions: Chloroquine can weaken the effect of Ampicillin. Primaquine is best not taken with Methotrexate and Chloramphenicol, while Erythromycin, anti-histamines and tricyclic anti-depressants should be avoided with Artemether. Quinine can also interact with digitalis, anti-coagulant warfarin and anti-diabetic pills.

Side effects: Anti-malarial medicines can cause various side effects, including nausea, diarrhoea, headaches, rashes, and blood disorders. Quinine can cause ringing in the ears, blurred vision, and hot flushes. Mefloquine can cause some people to experience dizziness, hallucinations, panic attacks, and depression. This drug should not be taken in early pregnancy or while you are breast-feeding; it may damage the foetus or cause adverse reactions in the baby.

Anthelminthic drugs

Anthelminthic medicines are used to eradicate worm infestations in the intestine, liver, lungs, and other organs of the body.

Major anthelminthics: Mebendazole, Piperazine, Levamisole, Pyrantel pamoate, Albendazole, Niclosamide, Praziquantel, Ivermectin, Diethylcarbamazine.

Safeguards: It is best to keep away from Piperazine should you have epilepsy. Levamisole must be avoided if you suffer from psoriatic joint disease, liver or kidney disease.

Side effects: Anthelminthics can sometimes produce diarrhoea, headaches, and dizziness. Albendazole may mar liver function; for those who require long treatment this may mean regular tests to monitor the liver.

Non-steroidal anti-inflammatory drugs (NSAIDS)

Primarily used for relief from pain and inflammation in muscles and joints, NSAIDs are probably the most commonly used medicines in the world. They work by blocking the production of prostaglandins, which are body chemicals that cause inflammation and contribute to the brain's perception of pain.

Major medicines: Aspirin, Paracetamol, Ibuprofen, Diclofenac, Ketoprofen, Naproxen, Nabumetone, Indomethacin, Nimesulide, Ketorolac, Prioxicam.

Benefits: Relief from aches and pains, arthritis, and other chronic inflammatory diseases. Low doses of Aspirin prevent blood from clotting and can ward off heart attacks and strokes, the two leading causes of death.

Safeguards: NSAIDs can irritate the stomach; it is therefore best to take them with food or milk. This restriction however does not apply to Paracetamol. Most physicians prefer to prescribe an ulcer-healing medicine to people who require prolonged treatment with NSAIDs. Alcohol must be avoided altogether, since it can also inflame the stomach lining.

People who have bronchial asthma or peptic ulcer must refrain from taking NSAIDs, since these drugs can worsen their illness. In both cases, Paracetamol is the safest analgesic. Low-dose Aspirin is not recommended for people who have a high content of uric acid or suffer from gout. Children below 12 years of age should not be given Aspirin or Nimesulide.

Drug interactions: NSAIDs can dampen the effect of several anti-hypertensive drugs, causing a rise in blood pressure. They also cause fluid retention, and Ibuprofen and Indomethacin increase the blood level of digoxin. This can have a serious bearing on people who have congestive heart failure. NSAIDs also inhibit blood clotting, and this can be dangerous in patients who are also taking anti-coagulant drugs.

Side effects: NSAIDs can produce inflammation, ulcers and bleeding from the stomach or intestine. They may also cause giddiness, rashes, and kidney and liver problems if taken for a prolonged period.

The risk of side effects is greatest in older people, in the disabled, and in people who are also taking the anti-inflammatory steroid, Prednisolone.

Anti-histamines (Anti-allergy drugs)

Anti-histamines block the release of histamine, a chemical released during allergic reactions.

Major medicines: Cetrizine, Loratidine, Terfenadine, Astemizole, Chloramphenicol, Cyproheptadine, Diphenhydramine, Promethazine, Triprolidine, Clemastine.

Benefits: Anti-histamines are used primarily to control symptoms of allergic conditions. They alleviate runny nose and sneezing in hay fever, can minimize rash and itching and atopic eczema, and allergic conjunctivitis. They also help relieve symptoms of drug allergy.

Safeguards: Anti-histamines can cause drowsiness and loss of concentration. It is therefore safer not to drink alcoholic beverages or perform tasks requiring mental alertness, such as driving. Persons with bronchial infection, glaucoma, or urinary tract difficulties should avoid using them, since their chemical effect can lead to worsening of these conditions.

Drug interactions: Loratidine can affect the function of several antibiotics, ulcer-healing drugs, and Ketaconazole, an anti-fungal drug. Chloramphenicol can react with the anti-epileptic Phenobarbitone. Terfenadine should not be taken with Ketaconazole.

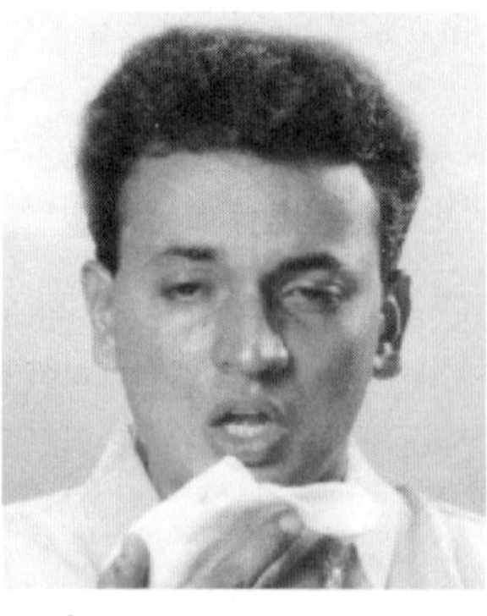

Side effects: The commonest side effects are drowsiness, loss of concentration, and dizziness. They also cause dryness of the mouth. Some anti-histamines increase the appetite and if taken over a long period, they can cause increase in weight.

Corticosteroids

Corticosteroids reduce inflammation by blocking the action of certain natural chemicals in the body.

Major medicines: Prednisolone, Beclomethasone, Betamethasone, Budesonide, Dexamethasone, Hydrocortisone.

Benefits: Corticosteroids play a useful role in bronchial asthma, allergy, rheumatoid arthritis, SLE, allergic rhinitis, sarcoidosis, idiopathic thrombocytopenic purpura, leukaemia and lymphoma.

Safeguards: People who have diabetes, high blood pressure, epilepsy, peptic ulcer, congestive heart failure, cirrhosis, any infection, glaucoma or hypothyroidism must be very careful while taking steroids, since these can complicate their illness.

Drug interactions: Corticosteroids dampen the effect of anti-epileptic medications. Women taking oral pills for contraception should watch their blood sugar since both steroids and oral pills can push it up. This restriction also applies to people who are taking thiazide diuretics.

Side effects: Prolonged steroid use can lead to weakening of bones, an increased susceptibility to infection, cataract, bruising, acute glaucoma, rise in blood pressure, headache, increase in weight, slow wound healing, and slow growth in children.

Anti-emetic drugs

Anti-emetic medications are used to treat nausea and vomiting. They act by suppressing the vomiting centre in the brain.

Major medicines: Domperidol, Metoclopromide, Promethazine, Cyclizine, Dimenhydrinate, Prochlorperazine, Trifluperazine, Ondansetron.

Safeguards: People who have epilepsy, obstruction in the digestive tract or extrapyramidal symptoms should avoid Domperidone and Metoclopromide, whereas Promethazine should be used with care if a person has prostate enlargement, glaucoma, or Parkinson's disease.

Drug interactions: Metoclopromide interferes with the absorption of the heart medicine, Digoxin. Concomitant use of Promethazine and Levadopa hampers the effect of both. Antacids reduce the absorption of Promethazine.

Side effects: Anti-emetic medications can cause constipation, drowsiness, tremor, repetitive twitching of small muscles of the face, tongue, eyes and neck, increase in the tone of muscles, and a flat expression on the face.

Ulcer-healing drugs

Ulcer-healing medications reduce the production of acid in the stomach.

Major medicines: *Proton pump inhibitors:* Pantoprazole, Lansoprazole, Omeprazole, Rabeprazole; *H_2 blockers:* Cimetidine, Ranitidine, Famotidine.

Benefits: Ulcer-healing medications heal ulcers, and relieve symptoms of dyspepsia and acid reflux.

Drug interactions: Antacids interfere with the absorption of Ranitidine. Omeprazole can slow down the metabolism of anti-coagulant Warfarin, Diazepam, and Aminophylline, prolonging their effect.

Side effects: Proton pump inhibitors can lead to headache, constipation, giddiness, blurred vision, rash and muscular pain. H_2 blockers can cause fatigue, dizziness and rash.

Bronchodilators

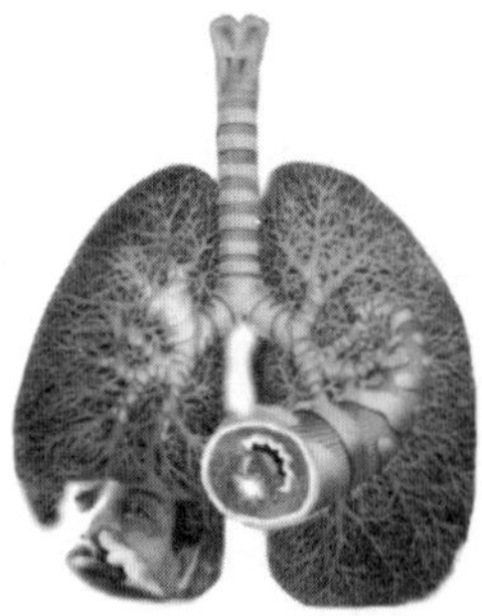

Bronchodilators expand the air passages (bronchial tubes) of the lungs.

Major medicines: Salbutamol, Salmeterol, Terbutaline, Ipatropium, Bambuterol, Theophylline, Aminophylline.

Benefits: Bronchodilators are used to treat asthma, bronchitis, emphysema, and other diseases that affect the lungs. They relieve symptoms such as wheezing, shortness of breath, coughing, and help restore the ability to breathe comfortably.

Safeguards: Persons with coronary heart disease, heart rhythm disorders, high blood pressure, epilepsy, and hyperthyroidism need to be very careful about using bronchodilators.

Drug interactions: Beta-blockers reduce the efficacy of Salbutamol, Salmeterol, and Terbutaline. If you take Aminophylline and Theophylline along with Salbutamol, Salmeterol, or Terbutaline, then potassium levels in the body can suffer a drop and this can upset the heart rhythm. Some anti-epileptics and the anti-tuberculous medicine, Rifampicin, reduce Theophylline's duration of effect.

Side effects: Salbutamol, Salmeterol, and Terbutaline can cause tremor, restlessness, palpitation and sleeplessness. Ipotropium can lead to dryness of mouth, blurred vision, and difficulty in passing urine. The use of Aminophylline and Theophylline may cause headache, nausea and palpitation.

Anti-hypertensive drugs

Anti-hypertensive medications are used to lower the blood pressure. They are of many types and are named according to the way they act within the body.

Major medicines: *Beta-blocker drugs:* Atenolol, Carvedilol, Labetalol, Metoprolol, Propranolol; *diuretics:* see page 42; *ACE inhibitor drugs:* Captopril, Enlapril, Lisinopril, Ramipril; *Angiotensin II blockers:* Losartan, Candesartan; *calcium channel blockers:* Amlodepine, Diltiazem, Nifedipine, Benidepine; *alpha blockers:* Prazosin, Terazosin; *other anti-hypertensives:* Clonidine, Methyldopa, Hydralazine, Nitroprusside.

Beta-blocker drugs

Commonly used in the treatment of high blood pressure, beta-blockers are also utilized to treat angina, rhythm disorders of the heart, and migraine.

Safeguards: Beta-blockers can worsen airway obstruction and should not be used by people who have asthma or chronic bronchitis. They can mask the symptoms of low blood sugar, and are therefore not suitable for diabetics who are on insulin. If you smoke, then also these medications are best not taken, because both smoking and beta-blockers reduce the blood flow to the limbs.

Never stop a beta-blocker drug abruptly. Sudden stoppage of beta-blockers can cause a rise in blood pressure, worsening of angina, and increase in the risk of a heart attack.

Side effects: If you are taking a beta-blocker, your hands and feet may feel cold because blood circulation in the extremities is reduced. Some people have difficulty in sleeping. Men may experience impotence, but normal sexual function usually returns when the drug is stopped.

ACE inhibitor drugs

ACE inhibitor drugs help lower blood pressure, ease the pressure on heart in congestive heart failure, and are useful in treatment of diabetic kidney disease.

Safeguards: ACE inhibitor drugs, especially when first used, can cause a sudden drop in blood pressure. One must therefore be extra careful and is best advised to take the first dose at bedtime. If you feel light-headed, get your blood pressure checked. Women, who are planning to conceive or are pregnant, should refrain from taking ACE inhibitors.

Drug interactions: Potassium-sparing diuretics and ACE inhibitor drugs, when taken together, can cause a rise in potassium in the body. This can build into a dangerous situation and must be watched against. Several medications enhance the effect of ACE inhibitors, but Indomethacin and antacids through differing mechanisms can reduce their efficacy.

Side effects: Some 20 per cent people develop a persistent dry cough within a few weeks of starting on ACE inhibitors. Some develop muscle cramps, diarrhoea, and others, urticaria, though rarely.

Angiotensin II blockers

Angiotensin II blockers ease the arteries and lower the blood pressure. They have the advantage that they do not cause the dry cough that ACE inhibitors sometimes cause.

Safeguards: Like ACE inhibitor drugs, they can also cause a sudden drop in blood pressure. Thus, if you feel light-headed, it is best to get the blood pressure checked. Angiotensin II blockers cannot be taken by people who have bad kidneys. Women planning to conceive should also avoid their use for reasons of safety.

Drug interactions: Taken with potassium-sparing diuretics, like Triametrene and Spironolactone, the body can have a surfeit of potassium.

Side effects: Some people suffer from dizziness, headache, insomnia and fatigue; surplus potassium can be a problem in persons taking potassium sparing diuretics.

Calcium channel blockers

Calcium channel blockers come handy both in the treatment of high blood pressure and angina. Some also help relieve migraine, others like Verapamil are used to treat heartbeat irregularities.

Safeguards: Never stop a calcium channel blocker drug abruptly, since this can cause a sudden worsening of angina.

Side effects: The most common side effects are headache, light-headedness, flushing, and swollen ankles. Some people also complain of constipation, nausea, palpitations, and excessive tiredness.

Diuretics

Diuretics increase the volume of urine and are used to remove excess fluid from the body. There are different types of diuretics which act at different sites along the kidney tubules.

Major medicines: *Thiazide drugs:* Chlorothiazide, Hydrochlorothiazide,

Indapamide, Chloratidine; *loop diuretics:* Furosemide, Bumetanide, Torasemide; *potassium-sparing diuretics:* Triamterene, Spironolactone, Amiloride; *others:* Acetazolamide.

Benefits: Diuretics are useful in the treatment of high blood pressure, congestive heart failure, and liver or kidney disorders associated with fluid accumulation in the body.

Safeguards: Diuretics are best taken early in the morning when the increase in urine is least likely to cause any inconvenience. The use of thiazides and loop diuretics leads to potassium deficit in the body, which must be bridged with potassium supplements. Thiazides can worsen diabetes, and thus should not be taken by people who have the disease. Diuretics are best avoided by individuals who have gout.

Drug interactions: NSAIDs weaken the efficacy of diuretics. Potassium deficit due to some diuretics can increase the toxicity of digitalis in patients of heart failure. Furosemide can accentuate the damage of aminoglycoside antibiotics on the hearing and balance apparatus of the inner ear.

Side effects: Thiazides and loop diuretics can cause excessive potassium loss, which can result in weakness, confusion, and heart rhythm irregularities. Thiazides can cause the skin to become sensitive to sunlight. Loop diuretics can lead to urinary problems in elderly men with enlarged prostate. Potassium-sparing diuretics can cause dryness of mouth, flatulence and nausea. Spironolactone may cause breast enlargement in men.

Angina-relieving drugs

Nitrate drugs are often used in conjunction with beta-blockers and ACE inhibitors in the treatment and prevention of angina pectoris. They relax the muscles of blood vessel walls, thereby dilating the arteries. As a result, blood supply to the heart muscle improves, workload on the heart is reduced, and chest pain is alleviated. However, they do not treat the underlying cause of angina—the narrowing down of the coronary arteries.

Major drugs: Nitroglycerin, Isosorbide dinitrate, Isosorbide mononitrate.

Safeguards: Alcoholic beverages should be completely avoided while using nitrates, since they can cause a precipitous drop in blood pressure. Persons with severe anaemia, recent head trauma, hyperthyroidism, glaucoma, or increased heart rate following a heart attack, should not take nitrates. Driving or other risk-related activities should be restricted if dizziness or faintness occur. Nitroglycerin taken in hot environments can cause excessively low blood pressure, while cold environments can increase the amount needed for full effectiveness.

Drug interactions: Nitroglycerin can interact adversely with several other drugs including many over-the-counter products for allergies, colds, and coughs; anti-hypertensive drugs; Aspirin; Dihydroergotamine; Diltiazem, and Heparin.

Side effects: The most common side effects of taking nitrates are facial flushing, headache, sudden drop in blood pressure, rapid heart beat, and palpitations. Diarrhoea and fainting may also occur.

Anti-diabetic medications

While insulin is a must in type-1 diabetes, a variety of drug options are available for treatment of type-2 diabetes.

Major medicines: Insulin; *sulfonylureas:* Chlorpropamide, Tolbutamide, Glibenclamide, Glipizide, Glyclazide, Glimepiride; *biguanides:* Metformin, Phenformin; *thiazolidinediones:* Pioglitazone, Rosiglitazone; *meglitinides:* Repaglinide; *alpha-glucosidase inhibitors:* Acarbose.

Safeguards: Doing anything that reduces your blood sugar after you have taken insulin or an oral hypoglycaemic pill, such as skipping a meal or exercising more than usual, can lead to low blood sugar.

Several anti-diabetic pills do not mix well with alcohol. Metformin can be particularly bad. If you take alcohol daily or occasionally overindulge, Metformin can produce lactic acidosis, making you feel sick.

If you need to take insulin, you must learn to recognize the symptoms of low blood sugar. Also you should train yourself on how to inject insulin, and measure your blood glucose levels at regular intervals during the day. This will help to check whether your insulin dose is at the correct level.

Drug interactions: Certain drugs, including decongestants, can boost the effects of sulfonylureas and this can lead to low blood sugar. Medications such as steroids, beta-blockers, niacin and the acne medication, Retino-A, can decrease the effectiveness of sulfonylureas. Talk with your doctor before taking any medication.

If you take the ulcer-healing medication, Cimetidine, your dose of Metformin may need to be lowered because of a possible drug interaction. Cimetidine can interfere with your kidney's ability to rid your body of Metformin, causing a build up of the drug and possible lactic acidosis.

Side effects: The most common side effect of sulfonylureas is low blood sugar, especially during the first four months of therapy when the decrease in your fasting blood sugar is most dramatic. You're at a much greater risk of developing hypoglycaemia if you have impaired liver or kidney function.

Metformin is generally quite tolerable, but in some people it can produce an unpleasant metallic taste in the mouth, nausea, loss of appetite, abdominal bloating, and gas.

Side effects of Thiazolidinediones may include swelling, weight gain and fatigue. A rare but serious side effect is liver injury. It is also important to have your liver checked every two months during the first year of therapy.

In the case of Acarbose, the gastrointestinal side effects can be bothersome. The drug can cause abdominal bloating, gas or diarrhoea. These effects usually occur during the first few weeks of taking the medication but decrease with time.

Anti-migraine drugs

Several medications can prove useful in the prevention and treatment of migraine headaches. If you suffer from frequent attacks, talk to your physician. Some medications, if taken regularly, can prevent attacks. For on and off attacks, ordinary pain-relief medication can help. There are also specific drugs like Ergotamine and Triptans which can relieve the symptoms during an acute attack.

Major medicines: *Preventive:* Amitryptiline, Flunarizine, Nifedipine, Propranolol, Verapamil; *pain-relief:* Paracetamol, Aspirin, Ergotamine, Sumatriptan, Rizatriptan.

Safeguards: Do not take any of the Triptan drugs if you have had Ergotamine within the last 24 hours. It can lead to a severe narrowing of the arteries.

If you suffer from high blood pressure or coronary artery disease, it is not safe to use Ergotamine, Sumatriptan, or Rizatriptan. People with Parkinson's disease should avoid using Flunarizine.

Drug interactions: Several anti-epileptics weaken the effect of Flunarizine. It is best to avoid the use of Methysergide or Ergotamine if you are taking beta-blockers, since the limb vessels can suffer severe narrowing. The use of oral pills with Ergotamine carries the risk of clotting in blood circulation.

Side effects: Each drug can lead to different side effects. Taking Flunarizine can cause drowsiness, weight gain, depression, and insomnia.

Propranolol may cause cold hands and feet and tiredness. Triptans can make you feel drowsy and can sometimes cause flushing, dizziness, tingling sensations, and chest pain. Use of Ergotamine may lead to muscle cramps, nausea, vomiting, abdominal pain, and diarrhoea.

Anti-convulsant drugs

Anti-convulsants reduce the activity of overexcited brain areas and reduce or eliminate seizures.

Major medicines: Carbamezapine, Ethosuximide, Gabapentin, Lamotrigine, Phenobarbital, Phenytoin, Primidone, Sodium valporate, Topiramate, Diazepam, Clonazepam.

Safeguards: You must be regular with the treatment. Abrupt stoppage of anti-convulsants can rapidly worsen seizures. Left untreated, prolonged seizures carry the risk of brain damage.

You may find that you have occasional seizures despite taking anti-convulsants. If this is the case, get in touch with your doctor. The dose of the medication may need to be adjusted or your doctor may like to try another drug.

Anti-convulsants carry a small but definite risk to the developing foetus. If you plan to have a baby, discuss it first with your doctor.

Drug interactions: Carbamezapine can weaken the effect of oral contraceptive pills, and this may make them lose their reliability. A number of medications, including ulcer-healing medicines, Verapamil, Erythromycin and anti-tuberculous drug Isoniazid increase the blood levels of Carbamezapine, leading to headaches, dizziness, and vomiting. A number of drugs can affect the blood levels and efficacy of Phenobarbital, Phenytoin, and Primidone, and it is best to consult your doctor before taking any other medication.

Side effects: Anti-convulsants can cause a number of side effects. consult your doctor if you have any sign of infection, a rash, bruising, or bleeding.

Phenytoin can cause gum hyperplasia, and also weaken the bones.

Most anti-convulsants cause drowsiness, impair concentration and induce lethargy. They can also affect memory and coordination.

Anxiolytics

Often referred to as tranquillizers, anxiolytic drugs quell anxiety by their chemical action on the anxiety centre of the brain. They are also useful in calming people who suffer from insomnia, depression, and panic attacks.

Major medicines: *Benzodiazepines:* Alprazolam, Chlordiazepoxide, Diazepam, Lorazepam, Clonazepam; Buspirone.

Safeguards: Anxiolytics can cause drowsiness, and therefore, it is safer not to drive. You should not drink alcohol while taking anxiolytics, because they increase the sedative effect.

Benzodiazepines should not be used for more than two or three weeks. If taken longer, the body may develop dependence towards them.

Drug interactions: Several medicines, such as phenothiazines, anti-epileptics, and analgesics can play up the sedative effect of anxiolytics.

Side effects: The commonest side effects are confusion, dizziness, lethargy and poor coordination. Some people suffer mild cognitive deficit, which affects their work efficiency. Others complain of weakened memory.

Some people also develop physical and psychological dependence. When medication is stopped, they show withdrawal symptoms. This risk increases if anxiolytics are taken for long, and the distress might last several weeks. Buspirone can cause headaches, nausea, and dizziness.

Anti-depressant drugs

Anti-depressants act by normalizing chemical activity in the emotional centres of the brain. There are at least seven different types, but the two most commonly used are the older tricyclic anti-depressants and the newer selective serotonin reuptake inhibitors (SSRIs).

Major medicines: *Tricyclic anti-depressants*: Amitriptyline, Nortriptyline, Imipramine, Trimipramine, Dothiepen, Doxepin, Clomipramine; *SSRIs:* Fluoxetine, Sertraline, Paroxetine, Fluvoxamine, Citalopram.

Safeguards: Anti-depressants do not work straight away. They take up to six weeks before their full benefit becomes obvious. The treatment should be continued for at least six months after the depression lifts off. Many people stop the medication much too early. This is a common reason why people do not get well.

Use of anti-depressants can cause drowsiness. It is therefore best not to drive or operate any machinery. Alcohol should be avoided, since it can further impair mental functions.

Drug interactions: A number of drugs, including oral pills, anti-diarrhoea drug Furazolidone, anti-Parkinson drug Levodopa, can influence the efficacy of tricyclic anti-depressants. Consult the doctor before taking any other medication. Some interactions can be downright dangerous.

Side effects: Tricyclic anti-depressants lead to dryness of mouth, constipation, blurred vision, tremor, fast heart-beats, sleepiness, and difficulty in passing urine. Men may experience impotence, or delayed ejaculation. Tricyclics are dangerous in overdose. They may cause seizures and heart rhythm irregularities.

SSRIs have a much lower rate of side effects. During the initial weeks of treatment, they may cause restlessness and anxiety—an effect that usually wears off. Some people suffer from indigestion, but relief can be found by taking the medicine with food. More seriously, they may interfere with sexual function. Other rare side effects include angina due to spasm in the coronary artery and alterations in blood clotting (prothrombin) time.

Anti-psychotic drugs

Antipsychotic medicines are used to treat schizophrenia and other severe psychiatric disorders. They alleviate hallucinations and other abnormal behavioural symptoms by regulating certain brain chemicals called neurotransmitters.

Major medicines: Risperidone, Flupenthixol, Olanzapine, Seroquel, Clozapine, Thioridazine, Trifluoperazine, Haloperidol, Chlorpromazine.

Safeguards: Anti-psychotic drugs help reduce symptoms in a large number of people suffering from schizophrenia. However, those who benefit often stop taking medication because they do not understand that they are ill or because of their unpleasant side effects. This can cause an acute worsening of symptoms.

Side effects: Minor side effects include dry mouth, blurred vision, constipation, dizziness, and drowsiness. Other side effects are more serious and debilitating. These may include muscle spasms or cramps, tremors, and tardive dyskinesia—an irreversible condition marked by uncontrollable and repeated jerking movements of the lips, mouth, eyelids and tongue.

Newer drugs, such as Clozapine, Olanzapine, and Risperidone, produce fewer side effects. However, clozapine can cause agranulocytosis, a serious blood disorder marked by acute fall in blood cells. For this reason, people taking Clozapine must have weekly tests to monitor their blood level.